What are those big cats?
They are lions!

Lions live in family groups.
These groups are called prides.

LIONS

by Mary Ellen Klukow

AMICUS | AMICUS INK

mane

spots

Look for these words and pictures as you read.

teeth

eyes

Look at the mane.
Only male lions have manes.

mane

Look at the spots.
Only young lions have spots.
They help the cubs hide.

spots

teeth

Look at the teeth.

They are sharp.

Lions use them to catch prey.

eyes

Look at the eyes.
Lions see well at night.

The pride sleeps.
Lions sleep for 20 hours a day!
They will hunt later.

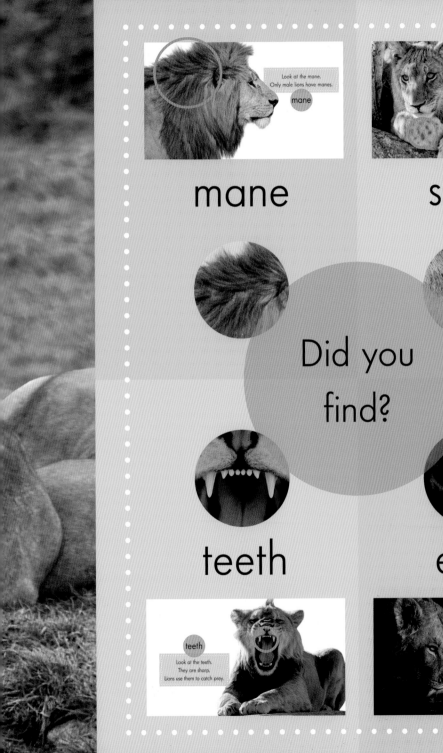

Look at the mane.
Only male lions have manes.

mane

Look at the spots.
Only young lions have spots.
They help the cubs hide.

spots

mane

spots

Did you find?

teeth

eyes

teeth

Look at the teeth.
They are sharp.
Lions use them to catch prey.

eyes

Look at the eyes.
Lions see well at night.

Spot is published by Amicus and Amicus Ink
P.O. Box 1329, Mankato, MN 56002
www.amicuspublishing.us

Library of Congress Cataloging-in-Publication Data
Names: Klukow, Mary Ellen, author.
Title: Lions / by Mary Ellen Klukow.
Description: Mankato, Minnesota : Amicus, [2020] | Series:
  Spot. African animals | Audience: K to Grade 3. |
Identifiers: LCCN 2018025818 (print) | LCCN 2018031330
  (ebook) | ISBN 9781681517247 (pdf) | ISBN
  9781681516424 (library binding) | ISBN 9781681524283
  (paperback) | ISBN 9781681517247 (ebook)
Subjects: LCSH: Lion--Africa--Juvenile literature.
Classification: LCC QL737.C23 (ebook) | LCC QL737.C23
  K598 2020 (print) | DDC 599.757--dc23
LC record available at https://lccn.loc.gov/2018025818

Printed in China

HC 10 9 8 7 6 5 4 3 2 1
PB 10 9 8 7 6 5 4 3 2 1

Wendy Dieker, editor
Deb Miner, series designer
Ciara Beitlich, book designer
Holly Young, photo researcher

Photos by Shutterstock/Stephanie
Periquet cover; iStock/GlobalP
1; Shutterstock/Maggy Meyer 3;
Shutterstock/oBebee 4–5; Getty/Alan
Hewitt 6–7; Adobe Stock/Ignatius
Tan 8–9; iStock/sboice 10–11; Alamy/
National Geographic/Beverly Joubert
12–13; Getty/John Dickson 14

LIONS